HIGH-STAKES HEISTS

CYBER HEISTS

KENNY ABDO

Fly!
An Imprint of Abdo Zoom
abdobooks.com

abdobooks.com

Published by Abdo Zoom, a division of ABDO, P.O. Box 398166, Minneapolis, Minnesota 55439. Copyright © 2025 by Abdo Consulting Group, Inc. International copyrights reserved in all countries. No part of this book may be reproduced in any form without written permission from the publisher. Fly!™ is a trademark and logo of Abdo Zoom.

Printed in the United States of America, North Mankato, Minnesota.
052024
092024

THIS BOOK CONTAINS RECYCLED MATERIALS

Photo Credits: Alamy, AP Images, Flickr, Getty Images, Shutterstock
Production Contributors: Kenny Abdo, Jennie Forsberg, Grace Hansen
Design Contributors: Candice Keimig, Neil Klinepier

Library of Congress Control Number: 2023948509

Publisher's Cataloging-in-Publication Data

Names: Abdo, Kenny, author.
Title: Cyber heists / by Kenny Abdo
Description: Minneapolis, Minnesota : Abdo Zoom, 2025 | Series: High-stakes heists | Includes online resources and index.
Identifiers: ISBN 9781098285715 (lib. bdg.) | ISBN 9781098286415 (ebook) | ISBN 9781098286767 (Read-to-me eBook)
Subjects: LCSH: Theft--Juvenile literature. | Computer crimes--Juvenile literature. | Internet crimes--Juvenile literature. | Securities theft--Juvenile literature. | Stealing--Juvenile literature. | Robbery--Juvenile literature.
Classification: DDC 364.162--dc23

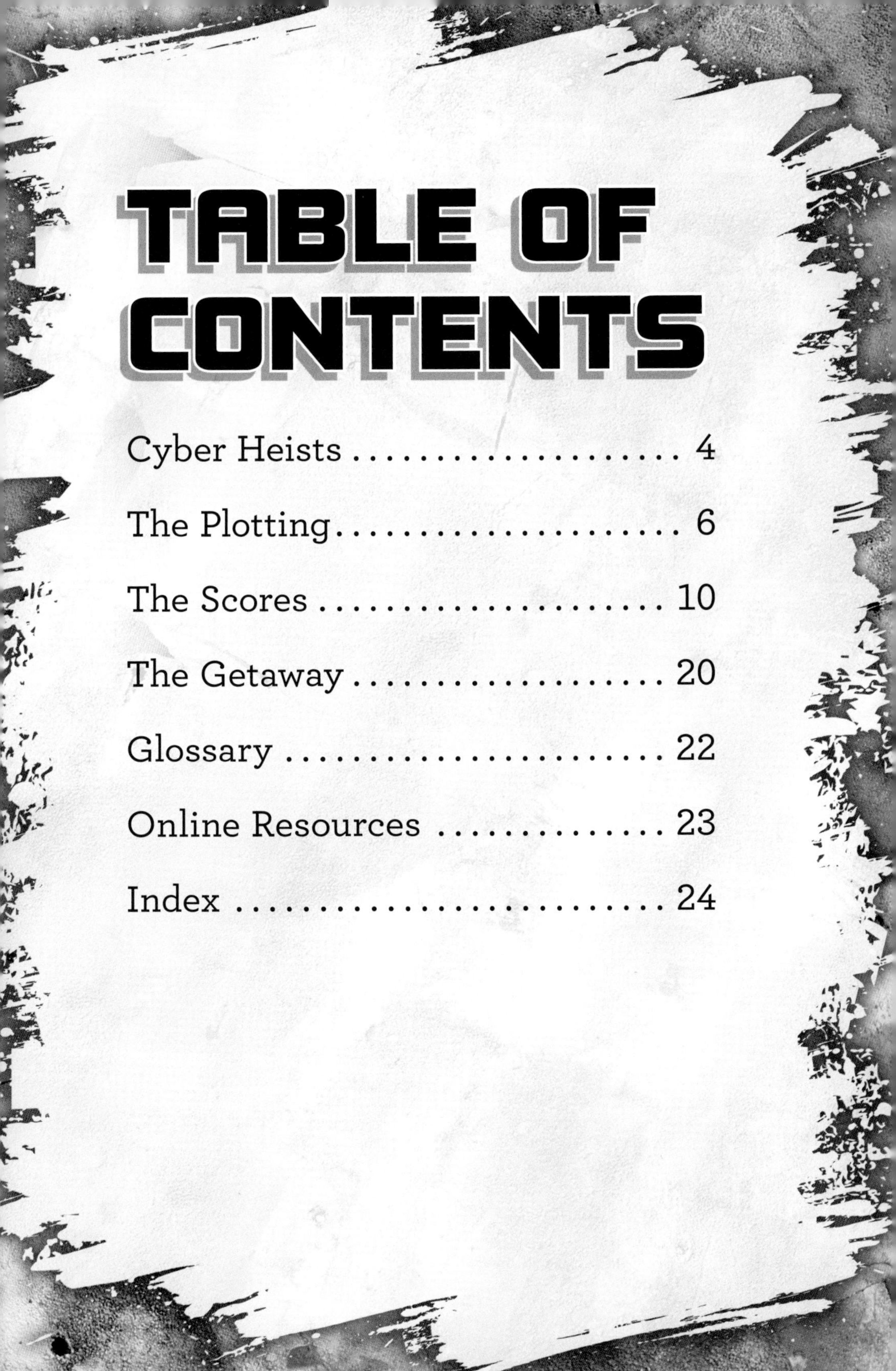

TABLE OF CONTENTS

CYBER HEISTS

Today, the internet has connected people throughout the world. Unfortunately, that includes **hackers** who surf the web looking for their next big score.

THE PLOTTING

The first internet **prototype**, ARPANET, was developed in the late 1960s. The internet as we know it launched January 1, 1983.

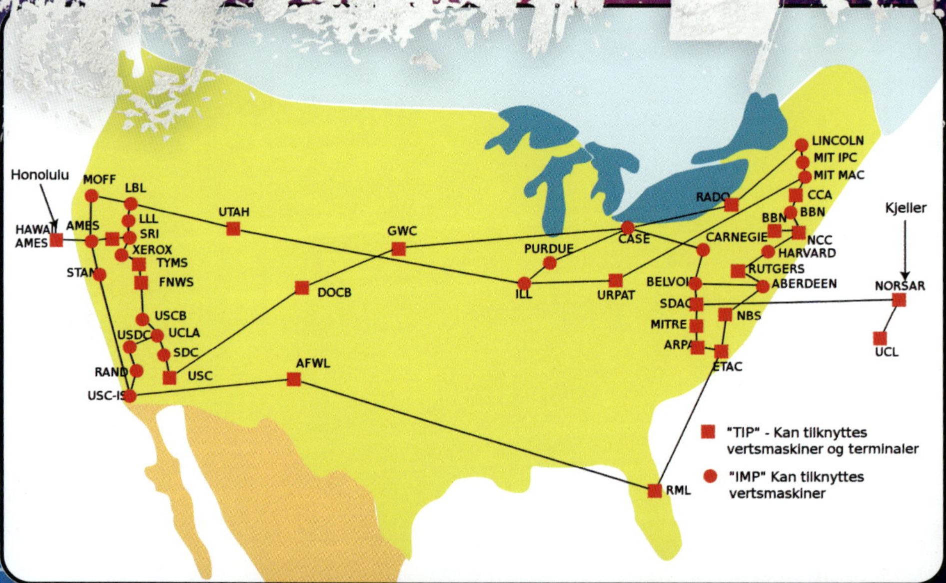

Xerox 80 paper
Healthe 1620

By 1988, Robert Tappan Morris released the Morris Worm. It is considered the first major cyber-attack. Triggering widespread trouble with computers, the virus caused more than $100,000 in damages.

Russian **hacker** Vladimir Levin broke into a Citibank computer in 1994. He was able to steal $10 million. Levin was eventually sentenced to three years in jail.

In 2005, Albert Gonzalez hacked into several retail computers. He stole more than 50 million credit card numbers. Gonzalez was arrested and sentenced to 20 years in prison.

A cyber attack hit companies such as Google in 2009. Chinese **hackers** stole trade secrets and sensitive information. The damage done was more than $100 million!

日報

京促保障　京強調符國際做法

Google風波
美僵局升級

■ 愈鬧愈大

Google擬撤出中國市場事件激起滔天巨浪，令中美關係再現暗湧。美國白宮指總統奧巴馬與美國政府一直支持互聯網自由；美國商務部部長駱家輝更敦促中國保障美資公司在華的營商環境安全。對此中國外交部昨則強調，中國管理互聯網的措施是國際通行做法，中方會向美方重申立場。但官方《環球時報》英文版則指，若Google真的退出中國市場，中國才會是輸家。

駱家輝

貝洛西

內地民眾使用互聯網愈加普遍，圖為女士們在餐廳使用無線上網。（法新社傳真）

白宮發言人昨表示，已與Google就撤出中國市場一事進行討論，但拒絕透露其體內容。發言人重申，奧巴馬與美國政府一直支持互聯網自由。美國商務部長駱家輝表示，Google遭黑客攻擊事件相當困擾美國政府及在中國營運的美國公司，他敦促中國保障在華的美資公司有一個安全的營商環境。

Google敢向中國當局說「不」，獲得美國各界支持，美國眾議院議長佩洛西對Google的聲明表示讚賞，認為是給企業界和各國政府樹立了榜樣。Google對手雅虎亦表示，雅虎與Google站在同一立場，譴責黑客的攻擊行為。

中方會向美方重申立場。

國務院新聞辦主任王晨昨早表示言，面對日益嚴峻的網絡安全形勢，政府部門亦要嚴查違法違規的網絡信息，吳邦國昨會見美國參議院代表時表示，彼此核心利益和重大關切。

京媒體：中國才是輸家

外交部反駁美方批評

The Mt. Gox **crypto exchange** was targeted in 2014. The hack caused a loss of 850,000 **bitcoins**. The company and its customers lost $3 billion. Mt. Gox recovered just around 20% of the stolen loot.

Cybercrime group Carbanak targeted banks worldwide. Between 2013 and 2016, the group stole more than $1 billion. The mastermind was arrested in 2018. But Carbanak heists have continued.

In 2017, a **ransomware** attack hit more than 200,000 computers. It demanded **bitcoins** from people in 150 countries. The losses are thought to be in the billions.

A Tokyo-based **cryptocurrency exchange** called Coincheck was looted in 2018. More than $560 million worth of crypto was stolen. Two years later, 30 people were charged for trading the stolen loot. It is still unknown who did the hack.

In 2020, **hackers** hijacked some famous Twitter accounts. Promoting a **bitcoin** scam, they tricked users to send money to fake addresses. In 2023, it was discovered a group of teens were behind it!

In 2023, cyber attackers targeted MGM Resorts in Las Vegas. It resulted in a $100 million loss. The thieves also took hotel guests' personal information, renaming the strip Lost Wages.

THE GETAWAY

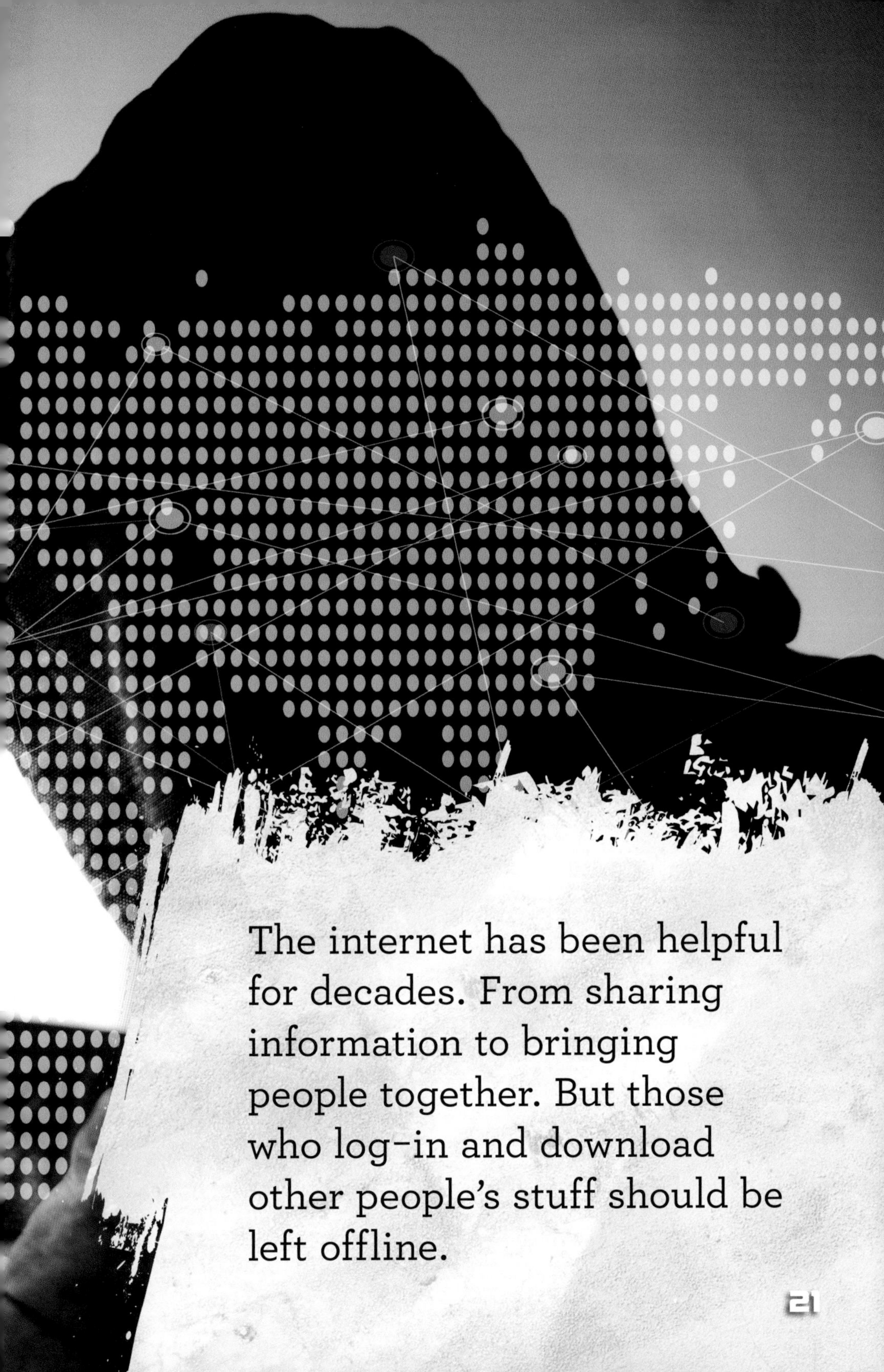

The internet has been helpful for decades. From sharing information to bringing people together. But those who log-in and download other people's stuff should be left offline.

GLOSSARY

bitcoin – a form of cryptocurrency. It allows people to buy, sell, and exchange without the use of banks or government agencies.

cryptocurrency – a type of digital currency, such as Bitcoin, that allows people to make payments through an online system.

exchange – a business that helps investors buy and sell digital currencies such as Bitcoin.

hacker – a person with the technical knowledge and skills to break into computer systems.

prototype – an early model of an idea or product.

ransomware – a software designed to block access to a computer system until a certain amount of money, or ransom, is paid.

ONLINE RESOURCES

Booklinks
NONFICTION NETWORK
FREE! ONLINE NONFICTION RESOURCES

To learn more about cyber heists, please visit **abdobooklinks.com** or scan this QR code. These links are routinely monitored and updated to provide the most current information available.

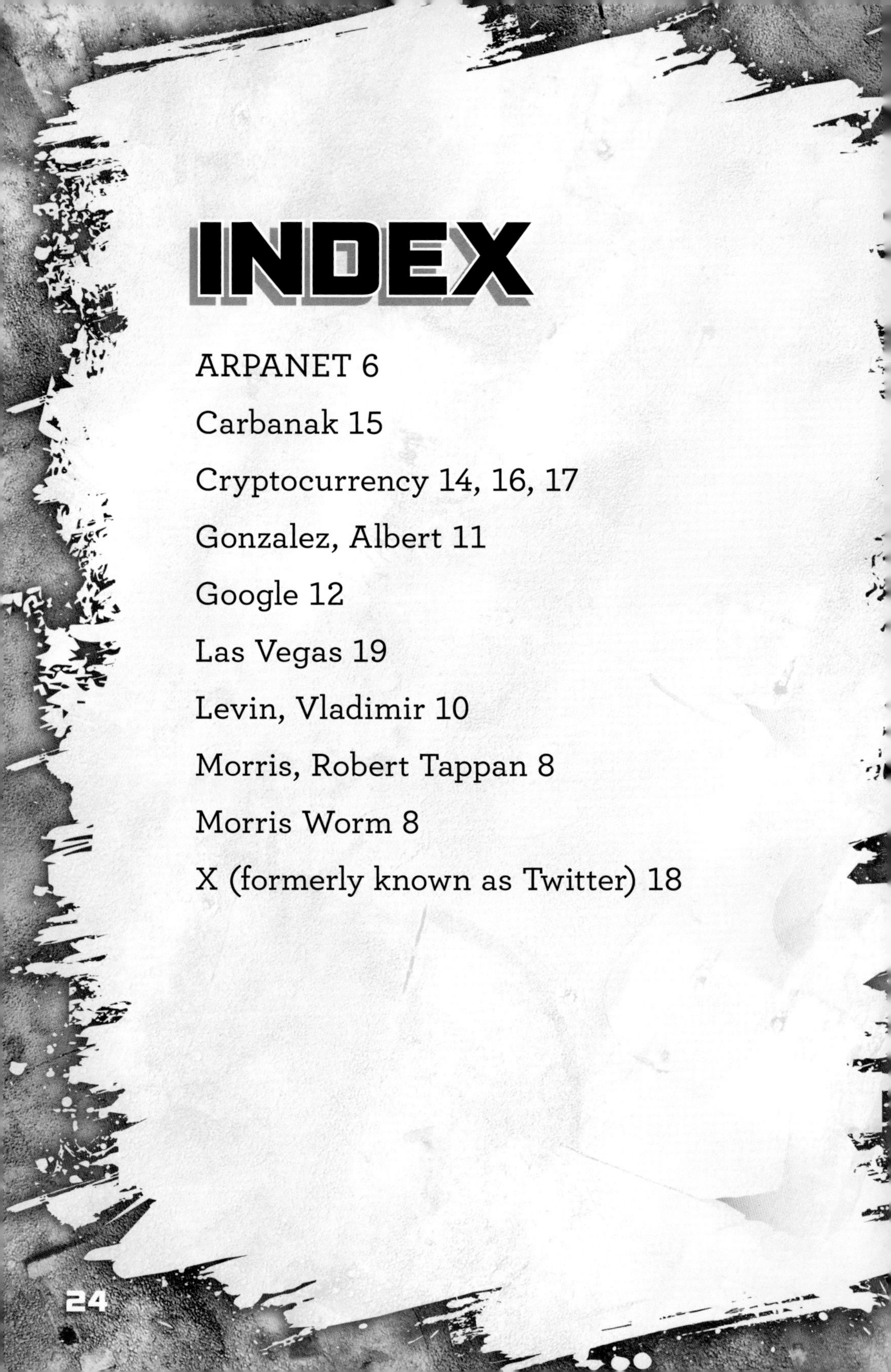

INDEX